REGARDING US

poems by

Terri Drake

Finishing Line Press
Georgetown, Kentucky

REGARDING US

ACKNOWLEDGMENTS

"The Time Will Come When You Shall See What the Hummingbird Sees" was
published in the *Citron Review*.

A heartfelt thanks to Maggie, Dion, Roxi, Chuck, and Farnaz whose
encouragement has kept me writing. Much gratitude to Gale Mead whose
photo restores Mead ranch to its former Eden. To Parry Murray, Gale Mead,
Kathleen Finneran, and Kim Johnson much love and thanks. Your friendship
keeps Jane alive for me.

Publisher: Leah Huete de Maines
Editor: Christen Kincaid
Cover Art: Gale Mead
Author Photo: EyeCatchLight Photography
Cover Design: Elizabeth Maines McCleavy

Order online: www.finishinglinepress.com
also available on amazon.com

Author inquiries and mail orders:
Finishing Line Press
PO Box 1626
Georgetown, Kentucky 40324
USA

Table of Contents

For Jane Mead
(1958-2019)

To love is to burn, to be on fire
—Jane Austen

REGARDING US

What I want for them to say:
they were both sorrowful and joyful.
They dreamed and they sang.
They sang when awake and when dreaming.
When all was lost, they sang.
When all was loss, they sang.

WHO I WAS

was rooted in who she was.
Now where is my existence?
As in some are ash, some *will be* ash.

RIVER, I LOVED HER

It's our secret.
The world goes on.
River, I sleep on your banks
then wake weeping
as if from a dream.

RIVER, IT BEGINS WITH HER BODY

and my body
appearing and reappearing,
knowing what happens
in the in between,
sentences building on sentences,
building on lifetimes,
seeing how her life was my life,
the chapter where everything happens.

I spent my young adulthood writing it,
my later adulthood finding its flaws.

I moved to the ocean,
its saltwater the exact saline content
of my blood. The ocean
where I became
who I didn't want to be
and your distance made you someone
I could have done without.

Yet in my darker moments,
it was still you I talked to.
Out of kinship and despair.

RIVER, WE MUST BEGIN

before the beginning,
with a grimness too grim to seem true.
Sentence after sentence of disquiet.
A protagonist unable to scream.
Bodies surfacing
she never knew were missing.
Subject of, subjected to.
She said *dark corridor,*
she said *alpine lake.*
She said *lodgepole pines*
torching the night.
She never said *me too.*

She stood in a heavy downpour,
chapter after chapter,
slogging toward anything,
never a foregone conclusion.

RIVER, WE ARE TWO BODIES

praying to the broken sky,
lying in the trench of the world,
star watching, cloud counting,
gazing at the dark bodies
of birds mending the air.

****

We are hemispheres shifting,
synapses snapping along mourning's shore.
There is fire in your hair.
You say wildflower, window frame.
I remember we baked bread.
After the first fire. Before the last.

THE GHOST HOUSE

she was born in
is larger than the present
ever was. Its eyelet curtains

flutter even when the wind
is still. In winter
the girl made snow angels

in the side yard
where the snow drifted
and the blizzards had their way.

There was no one to sing to,
this much is known.
It is no wonder

she carried on, mute.
There were elms and maples
and a weeping willow

nailing her to earth
and the abandoned pigeon coop
on whose slant roof

she waited for the world to start.

THE DARKER RIVER

banks lined
with pomegranate trees.
The hell you knew
was *this* world,
other people,

who kept the girl with brown hair mute.
Here, take this pomegranate,

each seed, a globe,
a possibility.

River, break the spell.

RIVER, I LOVED HER

in the shadow of the brown house.
We were bodies and poems.
Words woke us.
Took us elsewhere and together.
River, sing me a song for her.
When will this longing end?

****

I'm lost, river.
I don't know where you're going,
although I know where you always end:
in water so wide
the moon pulls it to shore
and it crashes over and over.

THE RIVER BEFORE, THE RIVER AFTER

Altered by earthquake,
river as loss, river as lost.
I went in once for love
and once for nothing.

If you follow it from Castle Rock,
you end up at the sea,
knowing its origin story.
It was never the same river
even once.
River of trance.
River of *what if* and *what for.*

By the time it reaches the Pacific,
it's hardly a river—
river of regrets, river of egrets
wading in drying out pools.

It can hardly believe it's still water.
In drought, even that will be taken.
River, I loved her.
We could have had forever
and it wouldn't be enough.

IOWA CITY

Cold front after cold front
colliding as the river ices over.

There was a brown house
and you lived there.

There was violence
that drew blood.

In the brown house
on the prairie

by the river you despaired
you'd ever write again.

The prairie's emptiness,
unwritten stanzas

trailing like the tail of a comet
in winter's darkness.

If I hear whispering in my ear
is it the cold wind

or you, the last poem
I will ever hear

HOWEVER FAR WE GET,

let's go further.
Whoever we'll be
won't be what's imagined.

Do oaks and madrones still hold
the hillside down?
What happens when
we can no longer imagine
ourselves together?

Who is going to write the next line
where the lost doe enters,
all landmarks blackened
and all you can think
is how will she ever survive

THE RIVER RUNS PAST US

unopposed
with or without us
by no coincidence.

Whoever answers, answer this:
will we discover
what the river means?
Or how to follow love
all the way to its source?

I KNOW WHAT THE RIVER KNOWS

moving past and beyond,
without mercy or thought,
what it carries.
I respond with my life,
language breaking and breaking
the shore. Mind removed,
once removed.

We are born gasping and wailing,
with wind blowing
across our bodies,
love fluttering up.

THE TIME WILL COME WHEN YOU SHALL SEE

what the hummingbird sees:
world as blur, body as fragile,
heart the fluttering of wings,
love hovering, body descending

GOLDEN HOUR ON THE RIVER

Glint of red hair,
hint of a smile,
bones down to the bones,
skin down to skin,
broken open photo
flash of wild rain.

ANOTHER COLD NOVEMBER

rain pouring
in the dark hills
after dusk,

in the morning
with the first birds.
I know nothing

of what matters most.
What can I say about rain
except that it comes down

in cold November, washing
the atmosphere clean.
There, now I can breathe.

Heart, come find me.
I am done with thinking—
its pale promises.

Tell me a story
that will set me on fire

IN THE END, IT'S ALL BODY AND STORY

Remember yesterday.
The sun room. The wind chimes.

Our backs are turned toward the river,
away from an ending.

In my dream you are both landing
and taking off.

I want to give you something
before you disappear.

You left me here
to write an ending

when you know
I've never been good at endings.

THE GHOST HOUSE, REVISITED

Still, the girl waits
on the slant roof
for the pigeons to reappear

in her loneliest of loneliness,
everything returned to her
in sequence, every pain

every joy, even the spider
and the moonlight between us

BY PHYSICS' LAW

Matter and anti-matter expanding
should have wiped us out.
Yet here we are.

I believe in the foxes and the apple orchard.
I believe the mind sets traps.
I believe in the wheat colored hills
and from the window you looked through
you meant to love me.

I believe in the distance and the breeze.
Did I say live oak?
I believe the live oak bears witness
to our losses. That our grief
is equal to our love.

As when our weeping
waters the marshes
and the dogs lick the salt
from our faces.

LUMINARIA

The paper lanterns
from your childhood New Mexico
illuminate the snow, the fear
that flames took everything
that mattered.

In my dream, your small dogs
are romping in the snow-brushed
sage at dusk. Before they cross over,

luminaria lighting the way,
they look back, making sure
you are following.

THE WAY

No compass no ruler
no internal GPS.
Others say perhaps
the way's how the sun
moves across the sky.

All I can say is *follow me.*
The red dirt is a path
to sprinkle ash on.
When everything is lost
at least the wind will carry you.

THOUGHT EXPERIMENT

To embody theory,
we start with the cellar.
You in it, skeletal.

human beings
are the only animal
for whom her own existence
is a problem.

I promise you
the dogs aren't agonizing.
Most likely they're chasing
the scent of a deer.

IF, AS FREUD SAYS

we are all instinctual drive,
lusty, rageful,

I can't promise
what will happen
when we're alone
in a room together.

THE RIVER'S PURPOSE

Coincidence is a coincidence
after all: it never meant
to do anything. Yet the wind

blows in from the ocean
and I held your hand
on the red earth's bank

like it was fate. Red earth,
red skin, against
a sun-burned sky.

The river curves around us
like it means to, a current
moving through the body's story
electrifying every nerve.

SOMETIMES THE BODY

is taken by surprise.
Where am I
and whose electrifying touch
has startled me from dream?

Or are the bony,
bird-like hands the dream?
You roll over,
the sheet rustling as it moves
across your body

WHAT DIDN'T HAPPEN

didn't survive
language, this much I know.
Dark horses, dark corners,
inarticulate litanies, unuttered sky.

We, who are born
of star particles,
nativities of the universe

slid forth into crickets cricketing
and other shrill anthems of the world.
The language before language

when our bodies pressed together
for a moment or eternity

WE DRIFT TOGETHER,

drift apart ….
when the world is done with us,
our bodies,
yet with our star eyes
shall we see God.

SOLITUDE

Solitude of all the bodies
dying in my arms.
I still feel their imprint, my keening.
We step into the river anyway.

Over and over.

A LOCK OF HAIR IN MY BUREAU,

so this is what you were?
We will never be a never together

in this life, the unspoken
never resurrected.
Our history outside language,

your keen ability to smell fear on the wind.
I brought home purple sage and heart's ease,
small offerings to the altar --

the argument against us
now as irrelevant as language
when you drop to your knees,

and no one, not even nature
can carry you back

AS IF MY LONGING COULD CONJURE

her out of the mists
over the ridge, back to the vineyards,
the dream body slipped
through the half-cracked door.

As if the ghost dogs come bounding
from the far childhood meadow.

She was loved. They were loved.
I go everywhere calling their names.

Notes:

"The Ghost House, Revisited" contains phrases and ideas from a section of Nietzche's "The Gay Science."

"Thought Experiment" the italicized stanza is a paraphrase of Erich Fromm

T erri Drake is a graduate of the Iowa Writers' Workshop. She is the author of *Regarding Us, At the Seams* (Bear Star Press) and *Singing in a Dark Language* (New CollAge Press). Her poems have appeared in *Crab Creek Review, the Chicago Quarterly Review, The Heavy Feather Review, Heartwood Literary Review, The Citron Review, the Laurel Review, the Ilanot Review Poets Reading the News,* and *Online Journal of Arts and Letters,* among others. She is a practicing psychoanalyst and lives in Santa Cruz, California.

www.ingramcontent.com/pod-product-compliance
Lightning Source LLC
LaVergne TN
LVHW041328080426
835513LV00008B/629